Ups And Downs
A Kid's Guide To Palma de Mallorca, Spain

Photography by John D. Weigand
Poetry by Penelope Dyan

Bellissima Publishing, LLC
Jamul, California
www.bellissimapublishing.com

Copyright © 2016 by Penny D. Weigand and John D. Weigand

All rights reserved. No part of this book may be reproduced or transmitted in any form or by any means, electronic or mechanical, including photocopying, recording, or by any other means, or by any information or storage retrieval system, without permission from the publisher.

ISBN 978-1-61477-263-7
First Edition

"What goes up must come down."

ISAAC NEWTON

Ups and Downs
Bellissima Publishing, LLC

Introduction

Things go up and things go down; and in Palma de Mallorca, Spain there are things that are up and things that are down, especially when you look at the topography and the landscape of this beautiful place! Palma de Mallorca is the capital of the Balearic Islands and the largest city in Mallorca. The name Palma dates back to the Roman settlement on the site of the present city. Originally settled during the Bronze Age, in the early middle ages, it was conquered by Arabs. After that, in 1229, it was conquered by King Jaime I, ruler of Valencia and Aragon, and became an important trade city. Then in the 1950's, it became a tourist destination.

Written by the award winning author, attorney and former teacher, Penelope Dyan, accompanied by the photographs of John D. Weigand, this 'learn to read' book with extra large print for little eyes, is the perfect size for a kid's backpack. Filled with word recognition, word repetition and rhyme, this book takes you on a journey through words and photography and lets you see some of what the author and photographer saw when they visited this unique and beautiful place. And if you want to see more, simply go to Bellssimavideo's YouTube channel and look for the free music video that goes along with this book and have even more learning fun!

Ups And Downs
Bellissima Publishing, LLC

Ups And Downs
A Kid's Guide To Palma de Mallorca, Spain

Photography by John D. Weigand
Poetry by Penelope Dyan

On the way up the hill
homes are what you see.
And your mom is as excited
as she can possibly be.

Bellver Castle can be seen
from the East.
For anyone's eyes this sight is a feast.
Mom says this day has a lot in store,
and you are again on your way
to see even more!

And the Real Cartuja de Valldemossa
lies ahead still,
sitting up there upon the hill.
Built as a royal residence,
and converted to a monastery in 1399,
the composer Chopin once stayed here,
composing music sublime.

You can take a long winding walk,
accompanied by a hedge of green.
Once up on the hill
there's so much to be seen!

In fact, if you only had the time,
you could stay and stay for hours;
and you could even take time
to smell the beautiful flowers!

And below what you learn
is now a museum (not a monastery)
there can be seen,
houses and fields,
and patches of green.

You go inside the monastery church
(still in use)
and you see a beautiful sight!
You wonder how you'll sleep tonight.
With all you that you have seen,
and with all
that's running through your head,
you think,
"How will I EVER sleep, once I crawl into bed?

Then you see the books!
It's a library!
Mom's eyes open wide!
Oh, how she would like to read,
EVERY single book inside!
She says, "You know my dear,
books ARE meant to last,
to teach each and every one of us,
all about OUR past.
And once you read the words inside,
from the mistakes of history,
you CANNOT hide!"

Next, the apothecary's room
catches the eyes of your dad,
who touts that for modern medicine
he really is glad!
Then Mom frowns at him,
and gives him a disapproving look.
She says, "I'll bet there's something
to be learned here,
in the apothecary's book!"

And necessity being the mother of
all invention,
there is a never ending winding candle,
that makes true that contention.
And right next to it
there appears to be a book,
into which your mother
really wants to look!

Then way too soon
back down the hill you go,
right into town.
You get something to eat.
And you look all around!

And Mom and Dad buy you
a fun wooden toy,
a blue mouse in a polka dotted dress,
that brings you great joy!
And then, they surprise you;
and for good measure,
they ALSO buy you
a wooden stork to treasure!

And suddenly, it seems
the day has turned to night,
and as you see the lights of
Cathedral de Santa Maria de Palma,
you know everything will be all right.
Yes, the day was busy.
Your mind is FILLED with stuff.
And you wonder if
(like your mom says)
of knowledge, there NEVER is enough!

"A room without books is like a body without a soul."

CICERO